Coast *of* California

FROM GOLDEN GATE TO THE GOLD COUNTRY

A TRAVEL PHOTO ART BOOK

LAINE CUNNINGHAM

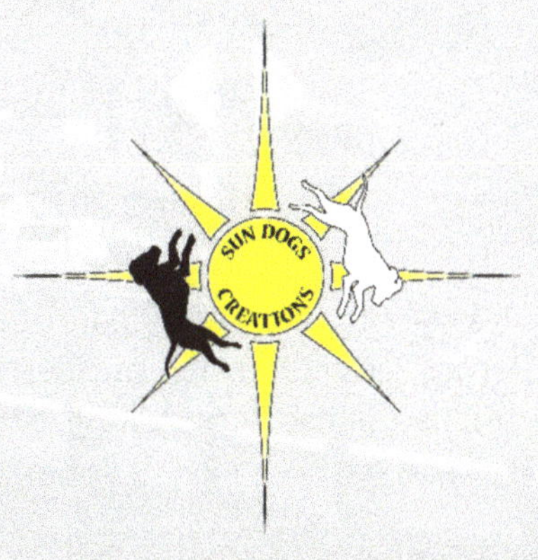

Coast of California

From Golden Gate to the Gold Country

A Travel Photo Art Book

Published by Sun Dogs Creations
Changing the World One Book at a Time
Print ISBN: 9781946732835

Cover Design by Angel Leya

THE TRAVEL PHOTO ART SERIES

Bikes of Berlin

Necropolises of New Orleans I & II

Ruins of Rome I & II

Ancients of Assisi I & II

Panoramas of Portugal

Nuances of New York

Glimpses of Germany

Impressions of Italy

Altitudes of the Alps

Coast of California

Utopia of the Unicorn

Knights Through the Ages

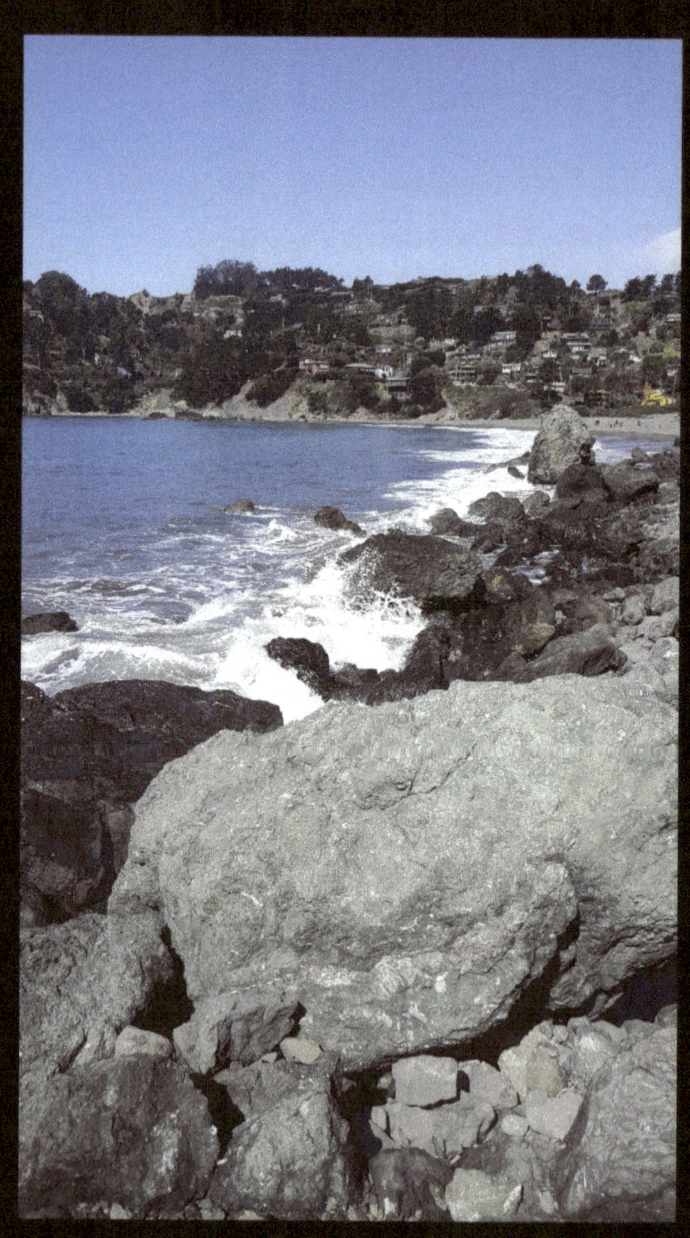

MANATEE

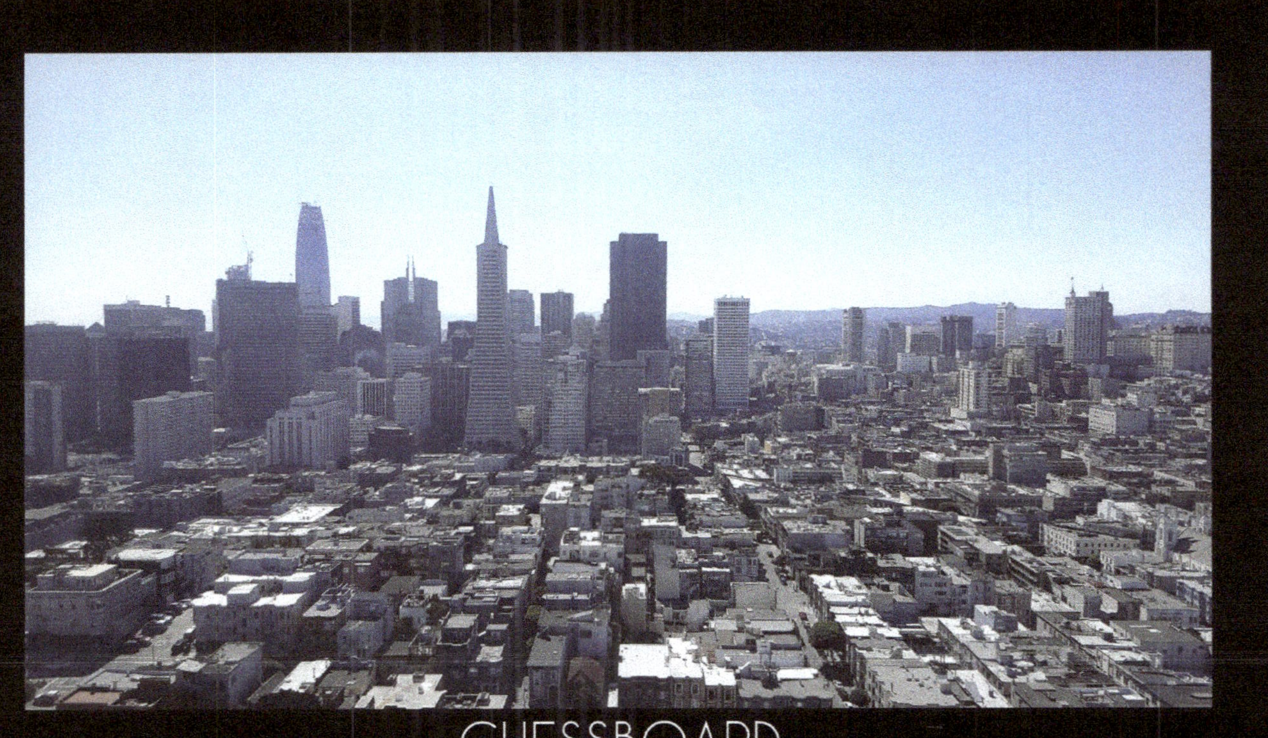

CHESSBOARD

EXPECTING

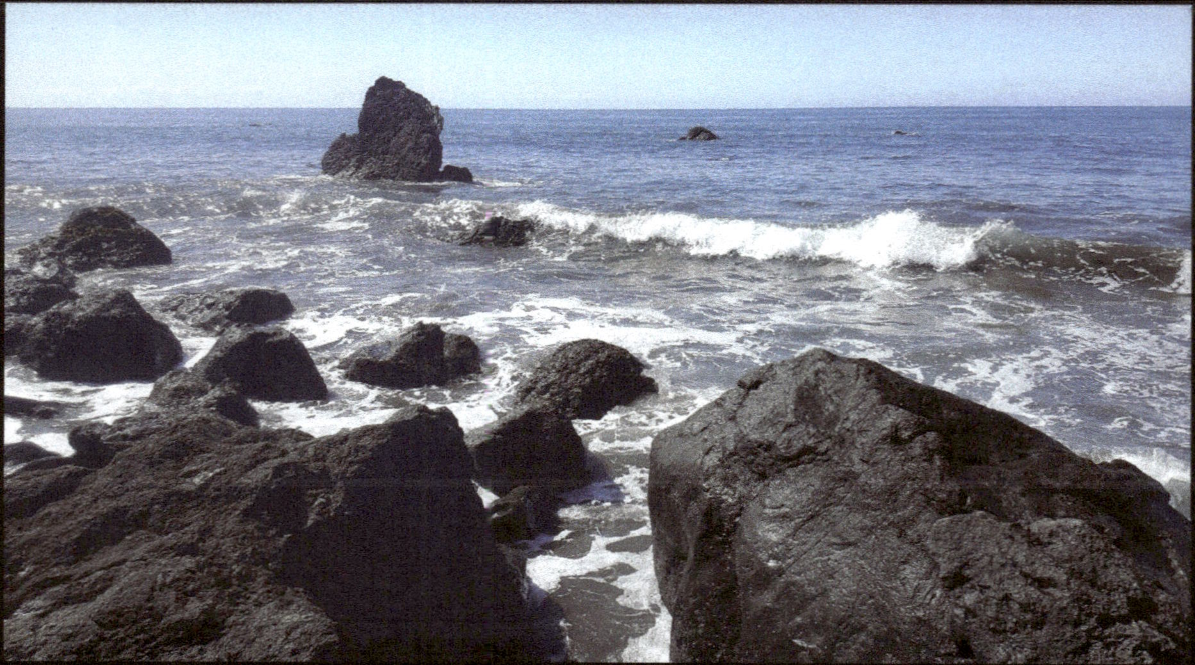

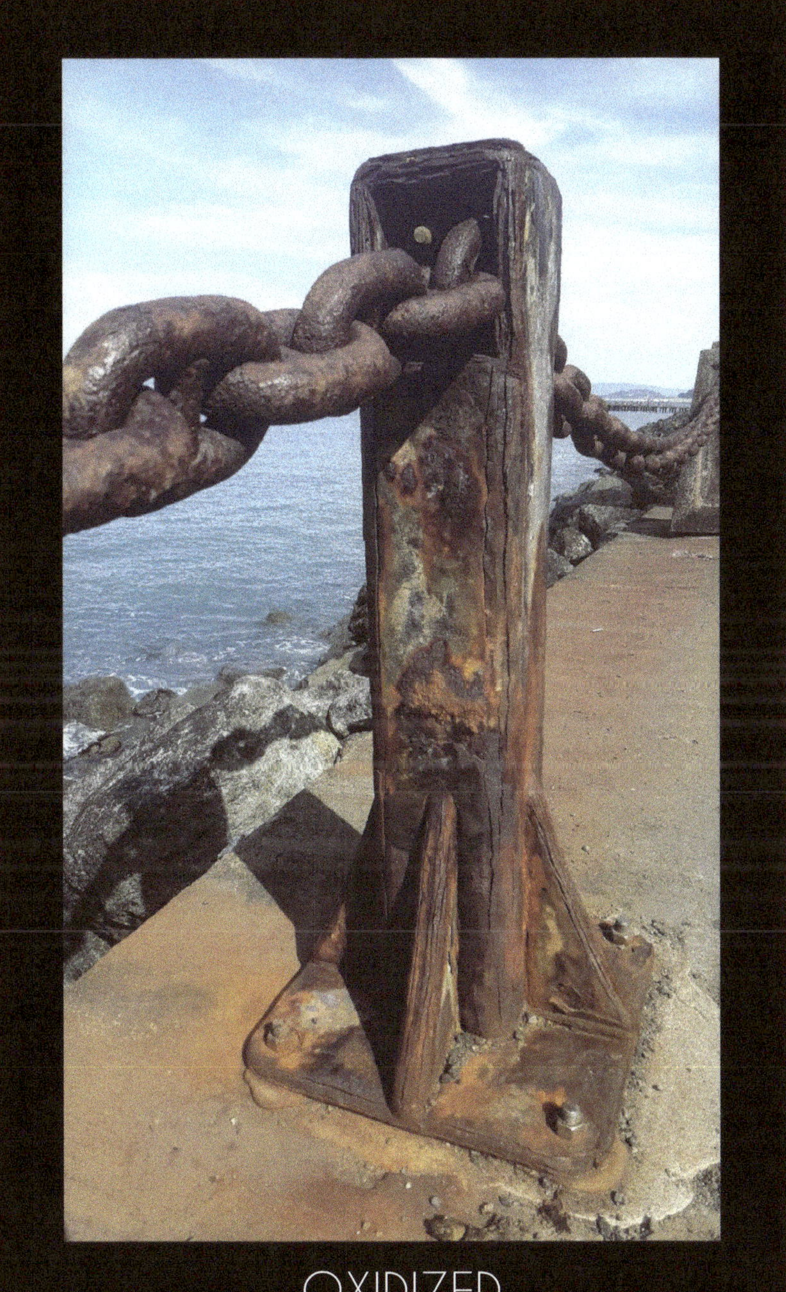

OXIDIZED

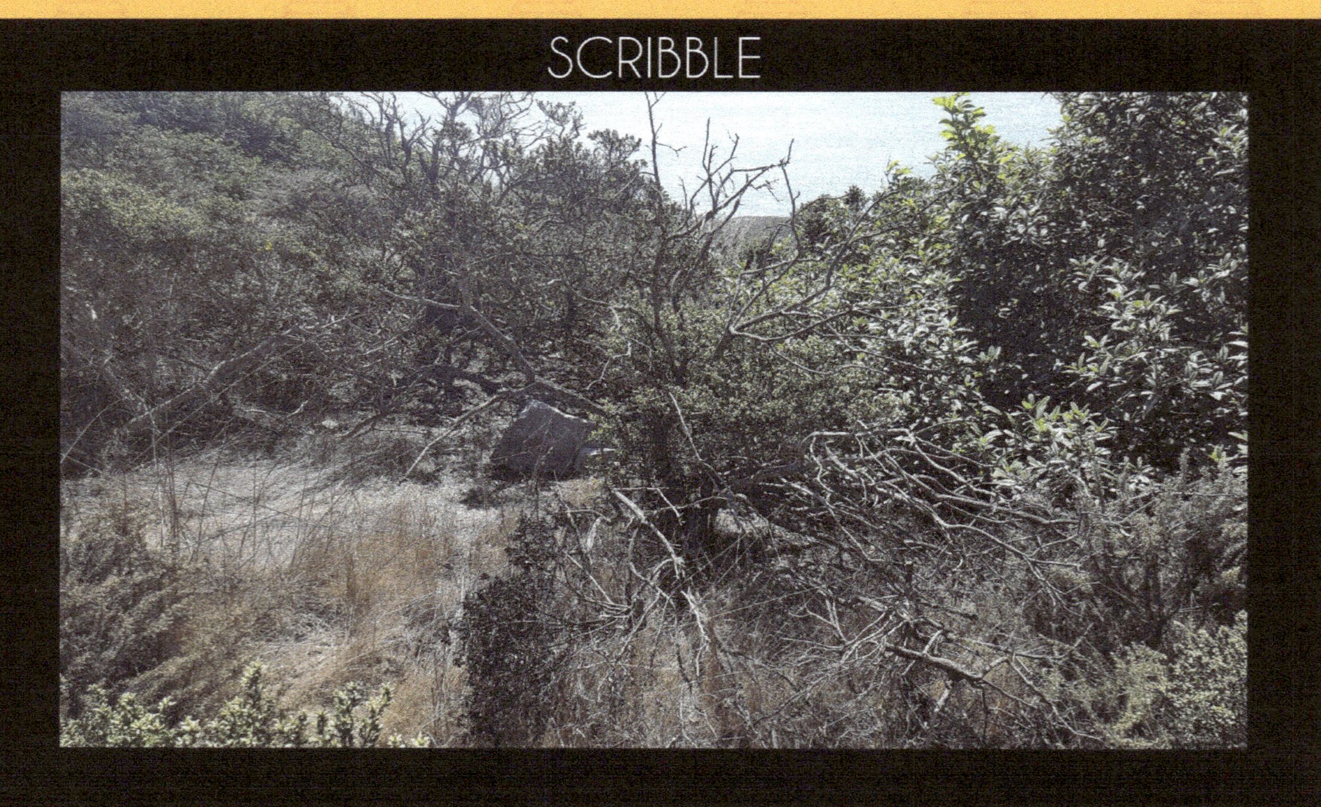

SCRIBBLE

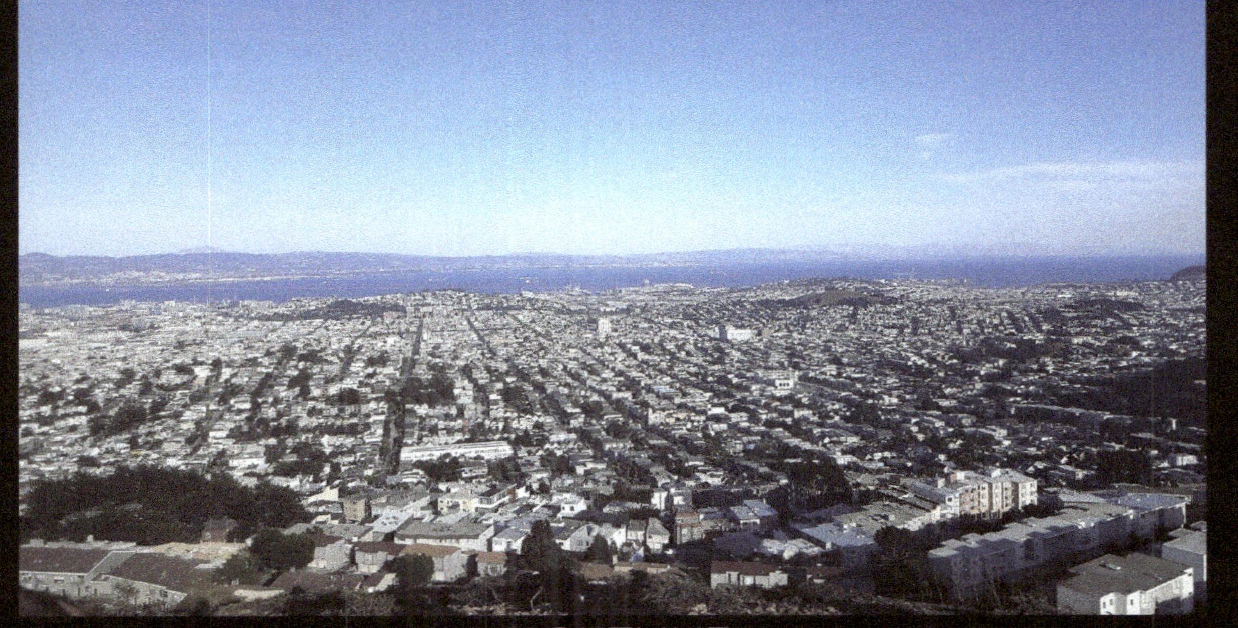
SIGHTLINE

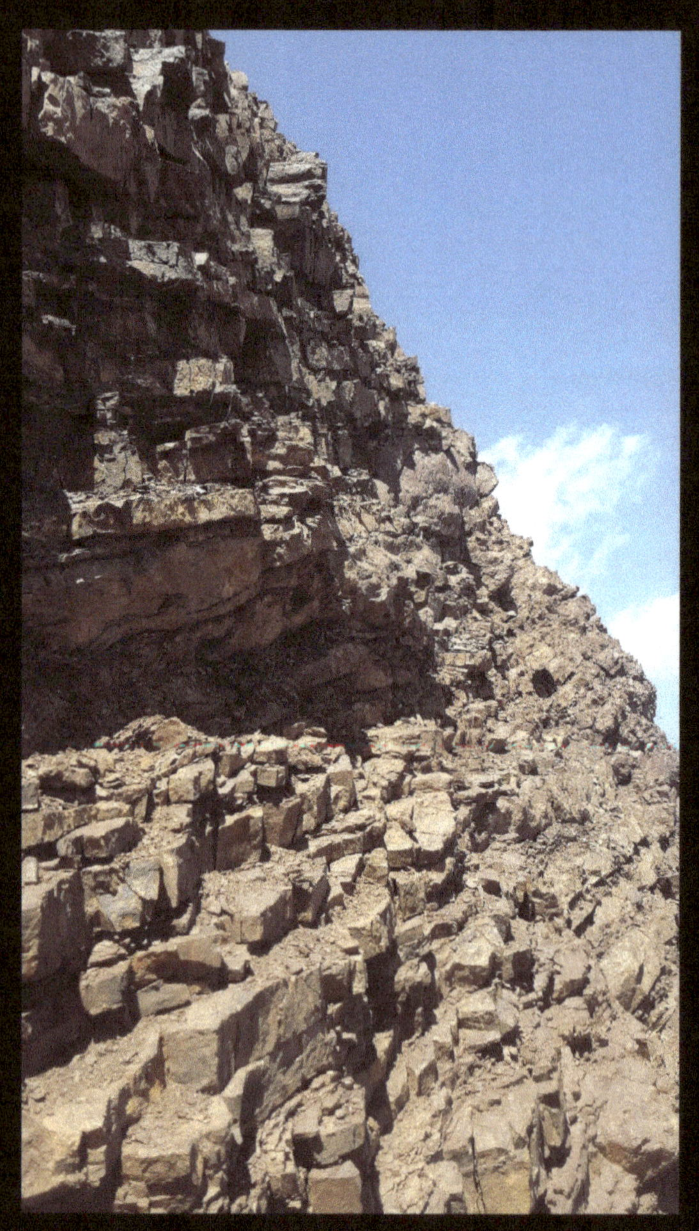

MOUNTAINEER

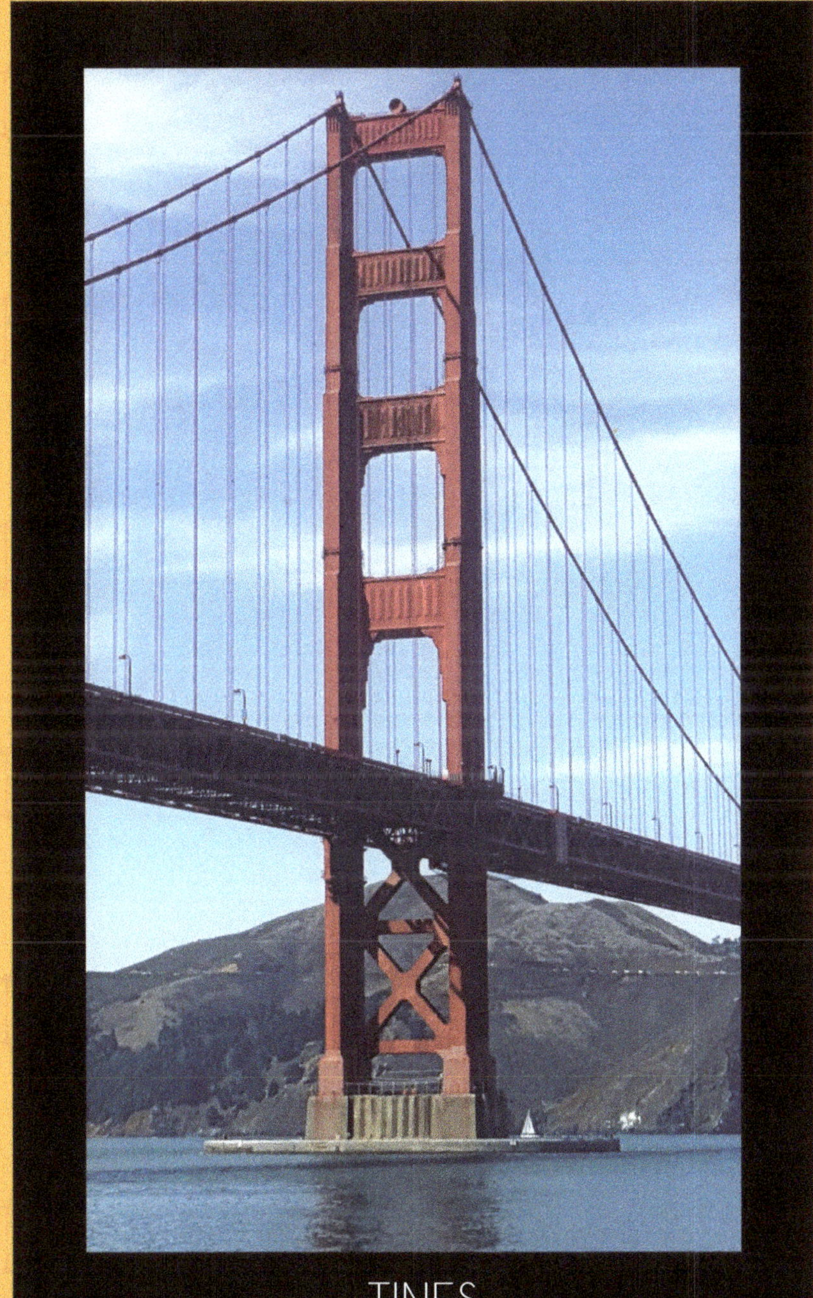
TINES

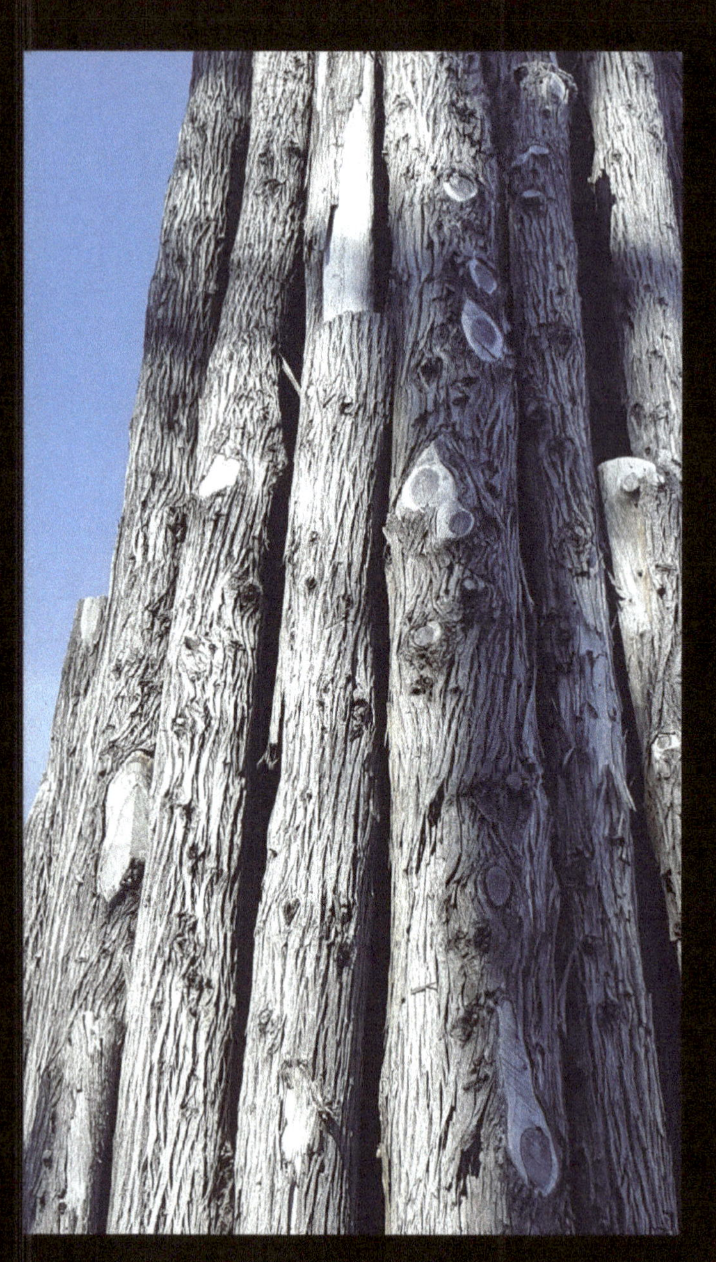

TWIZZLERS

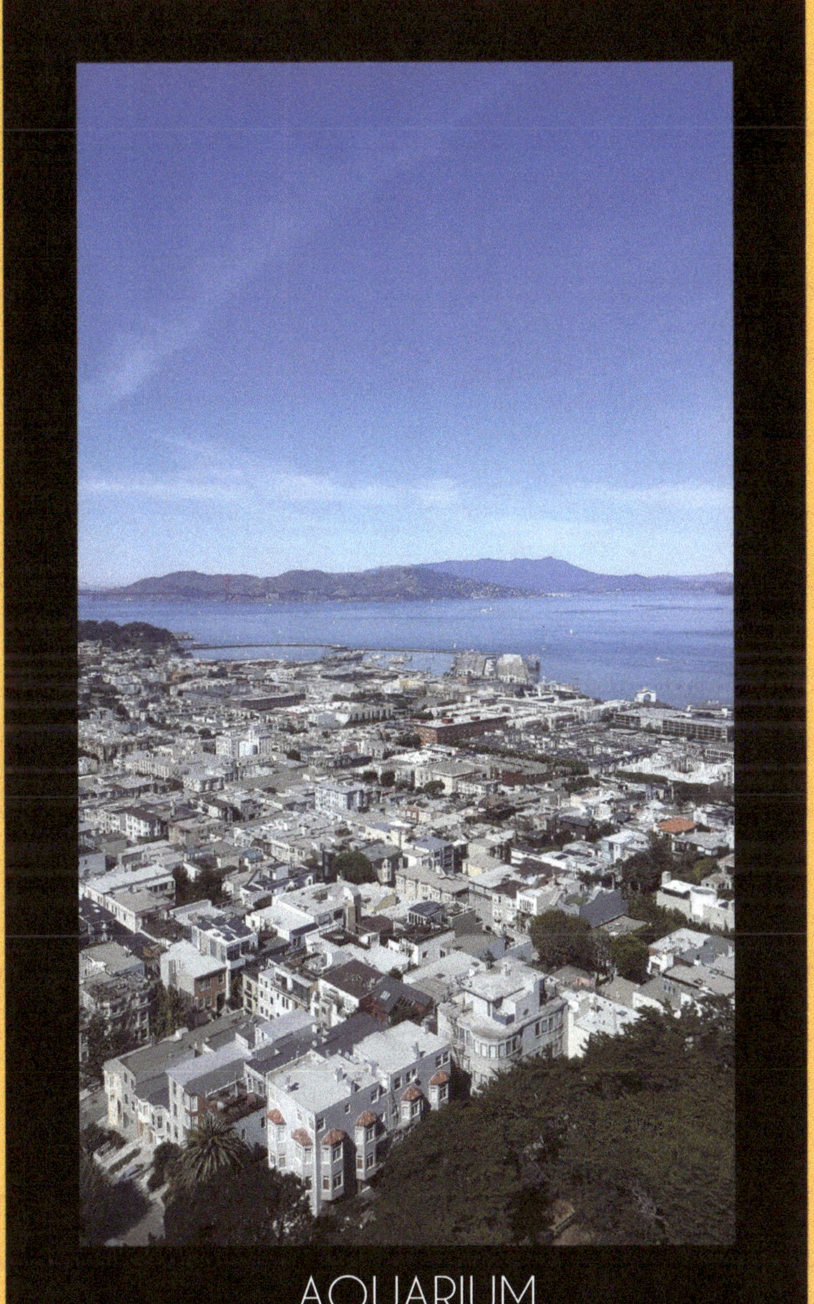

AQUARIUM

HELLO GOODBYE

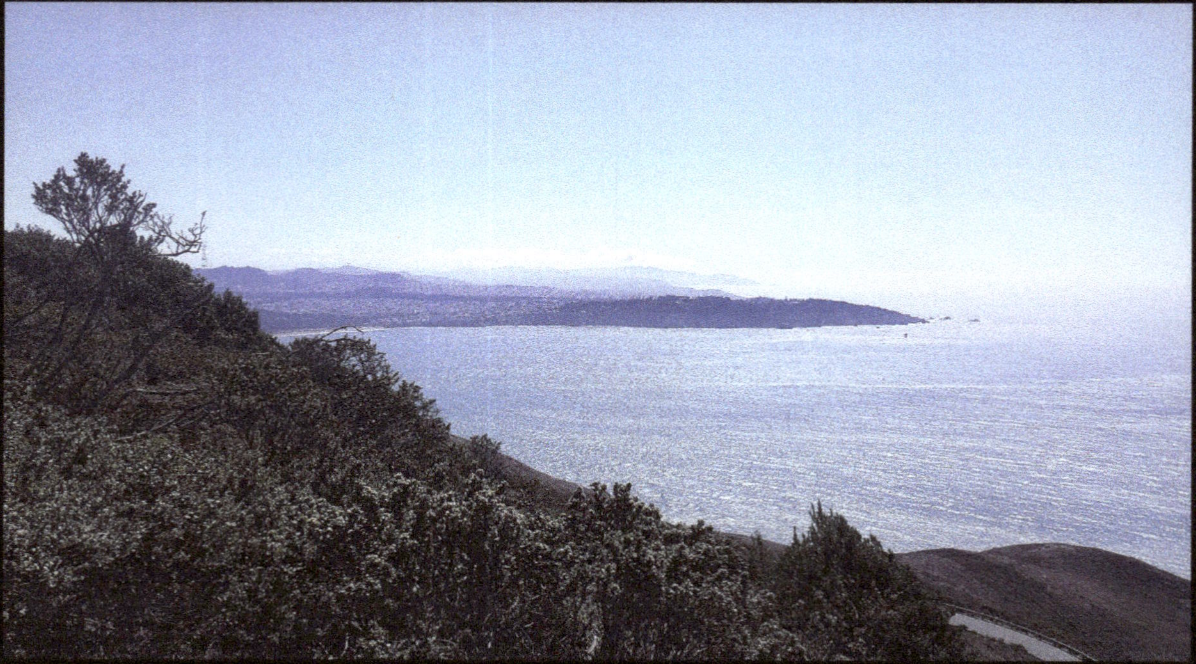

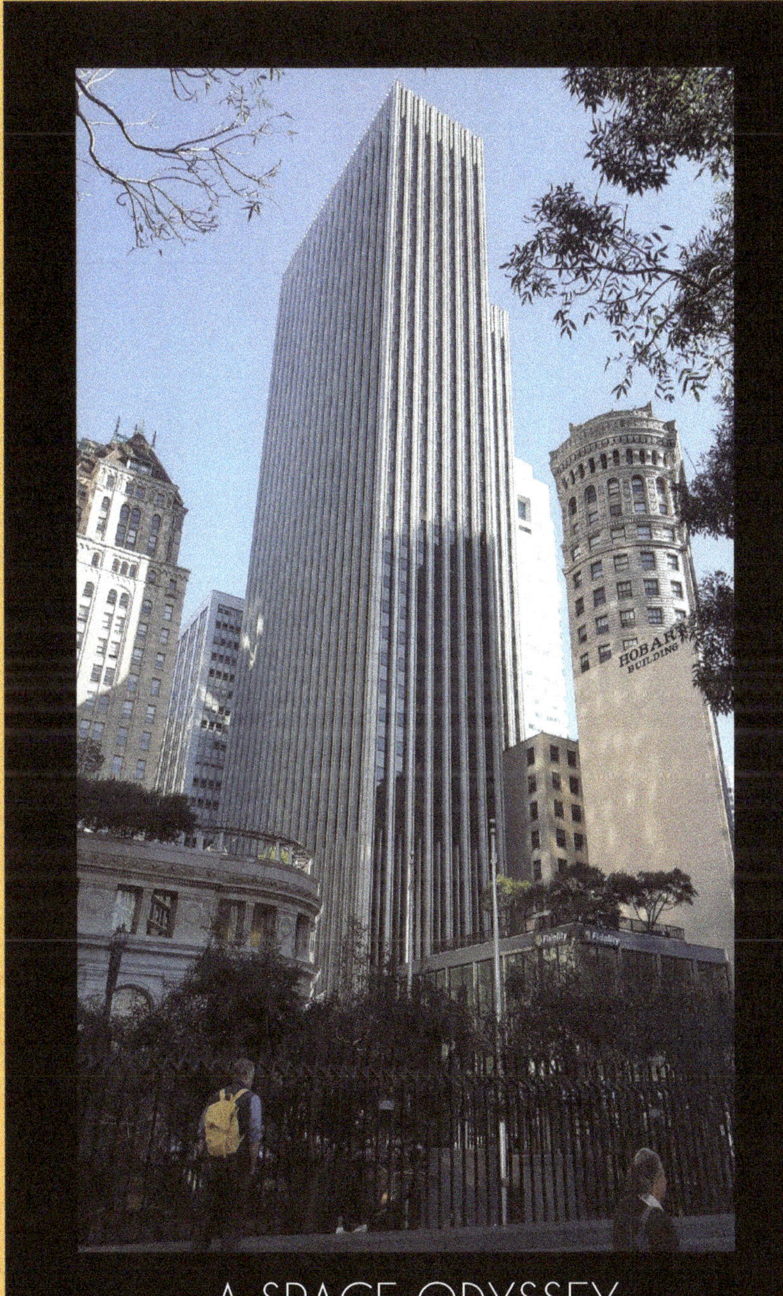

HOBART
BUILDING
A SPACE ODYSSEY

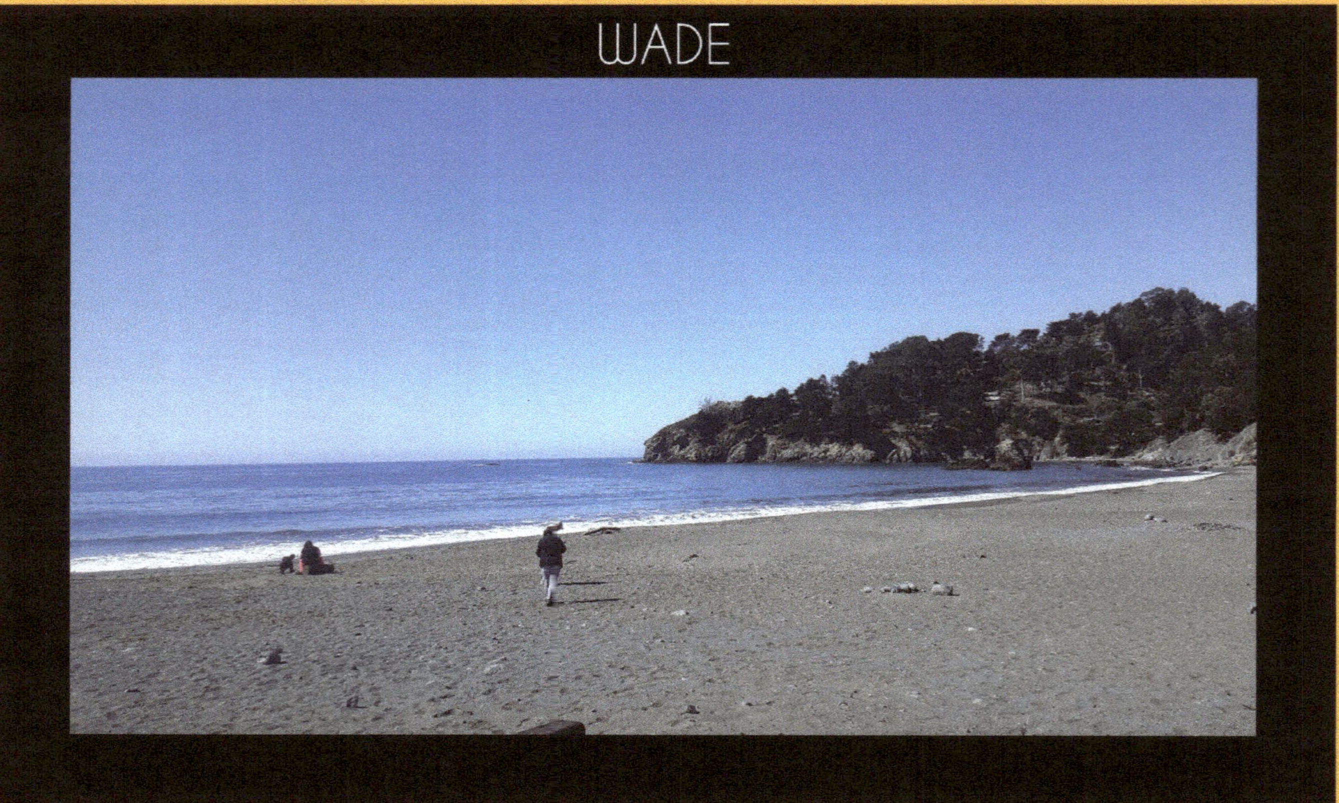
WADE

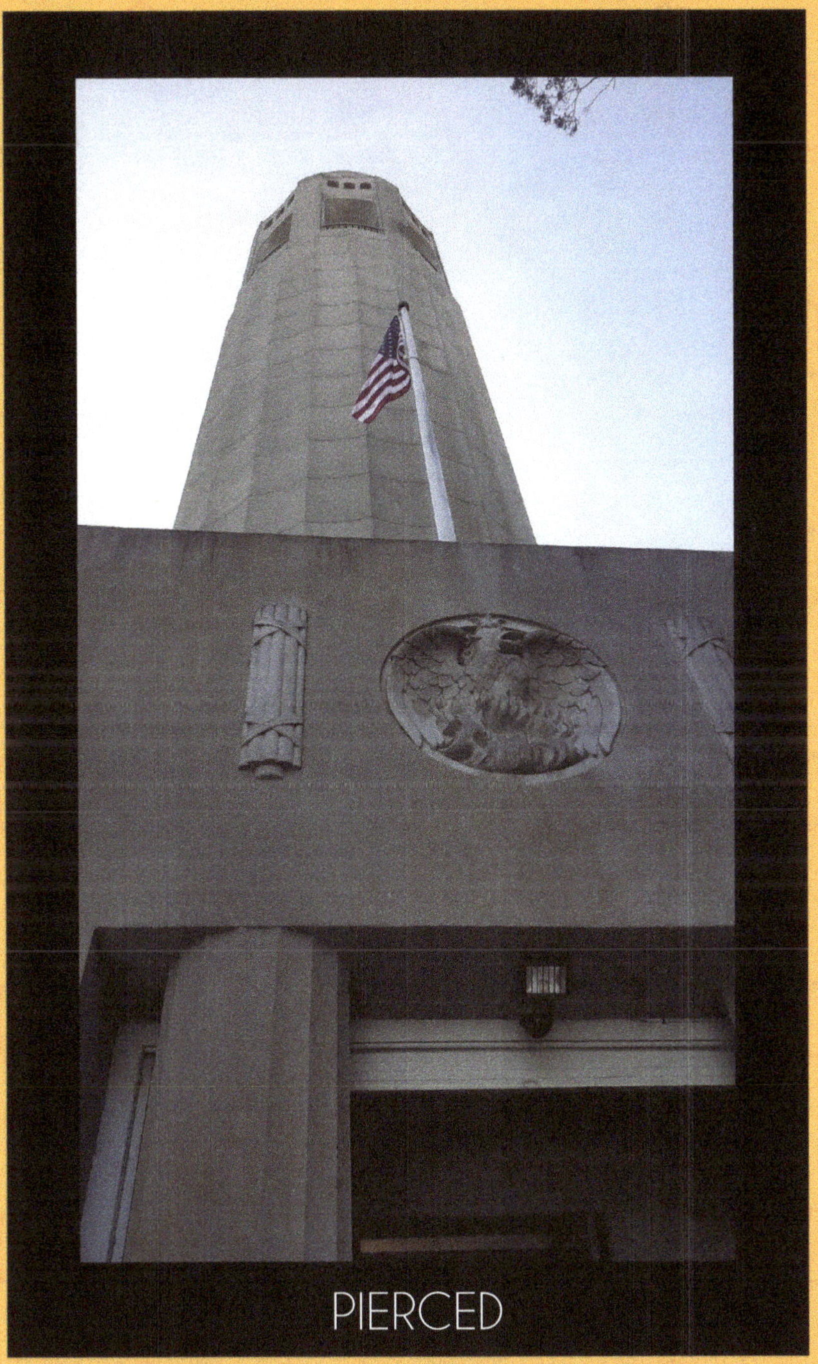

PIERCED

VIOLET LIGHT

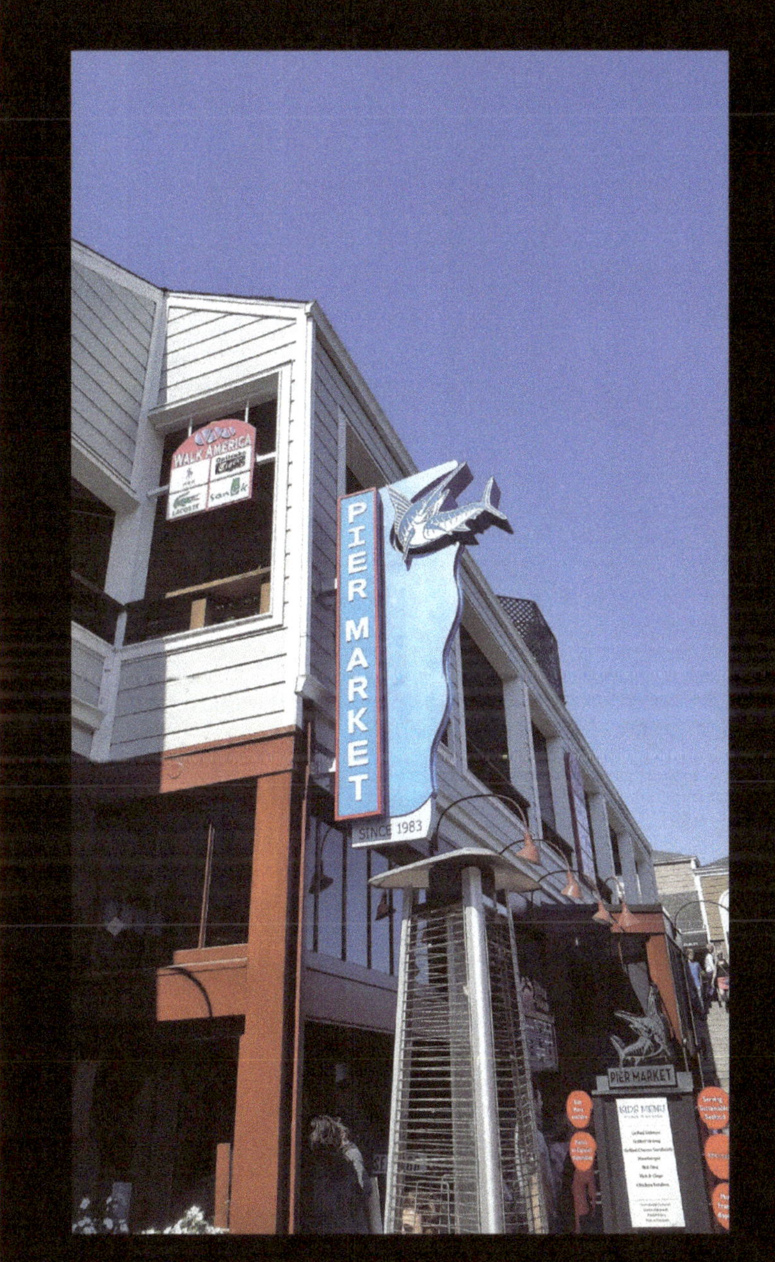

BROADSWORD

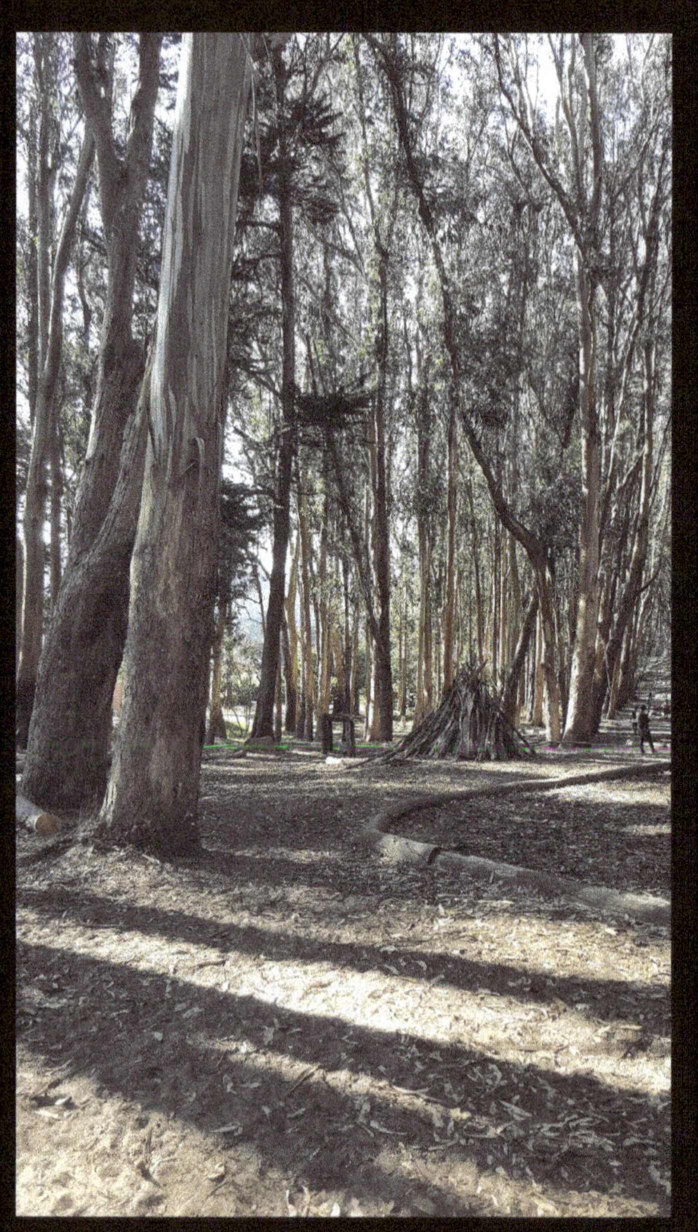

BATHING TRUNKS

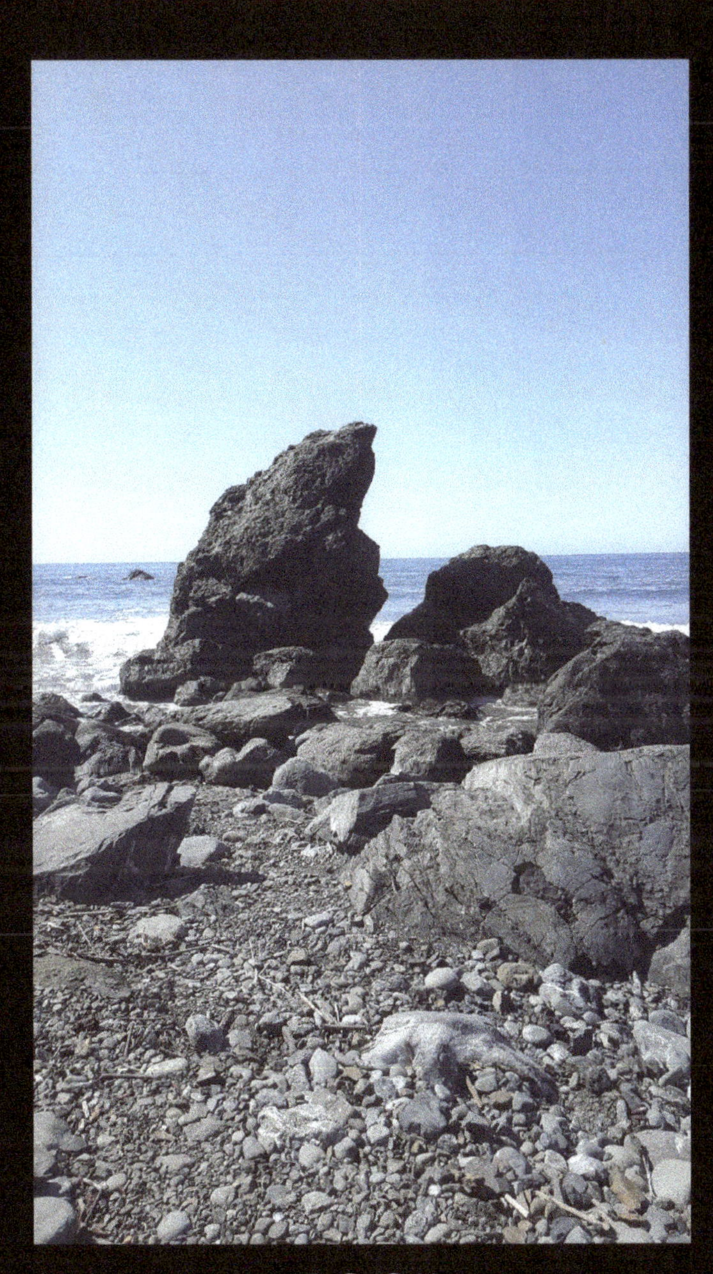

ROOK

AZURE BREEZE

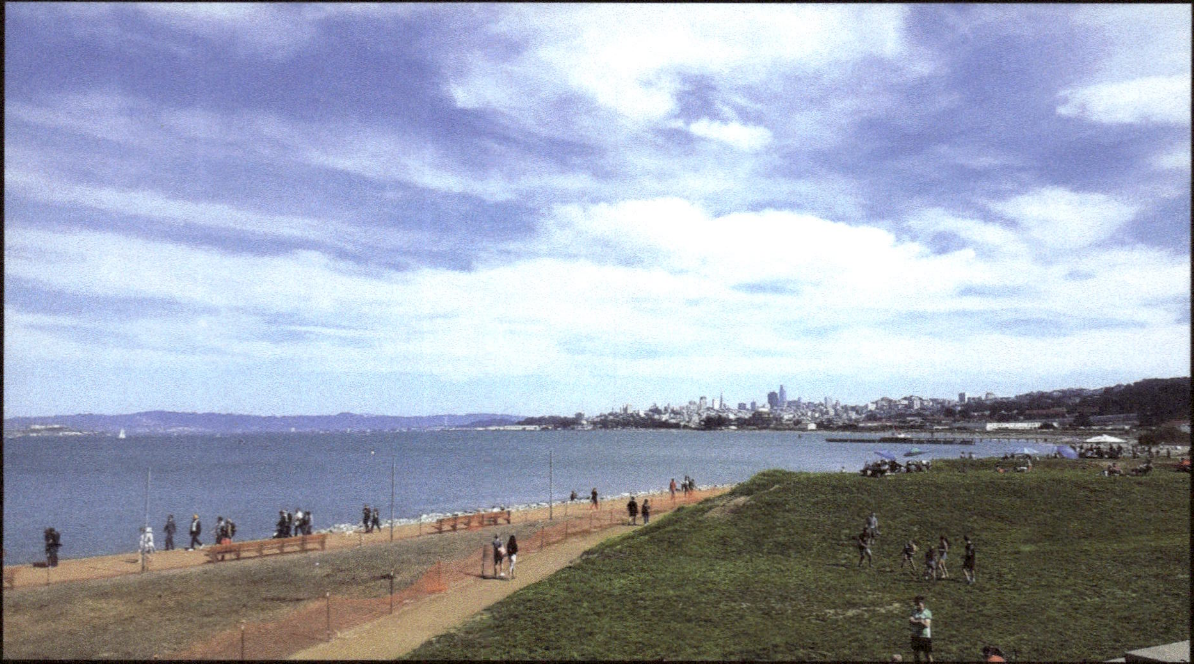

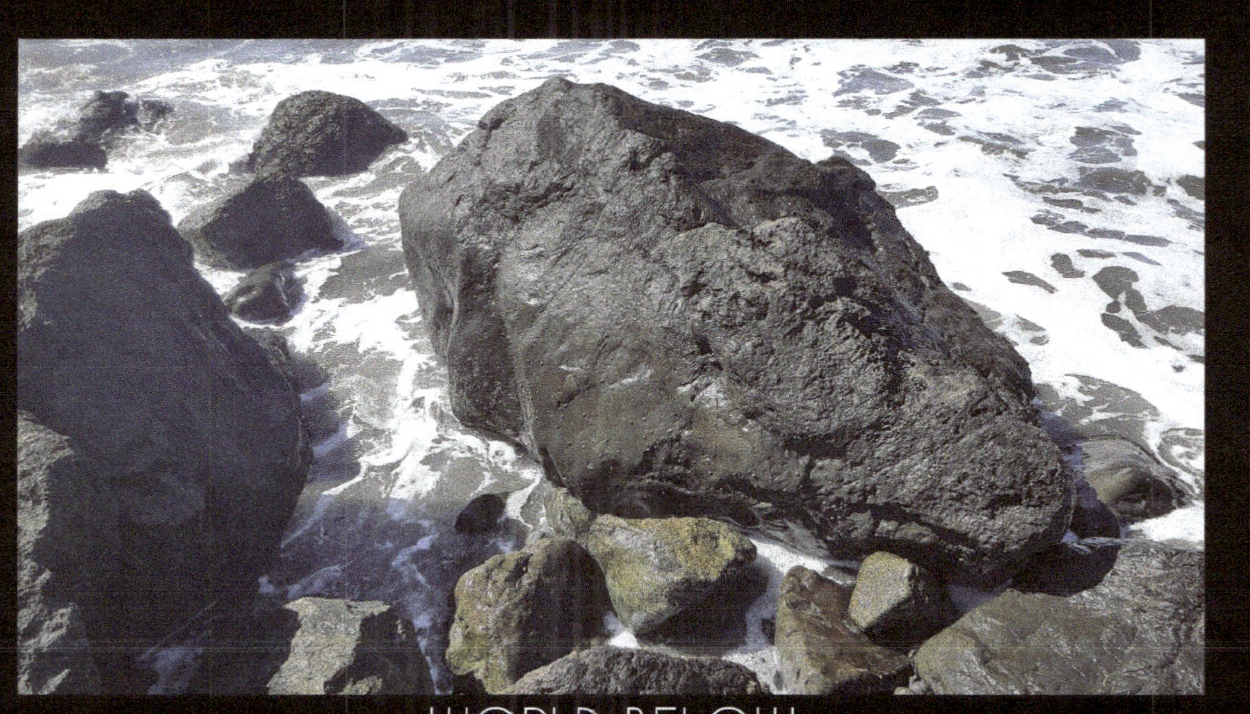
WORLD BELOW

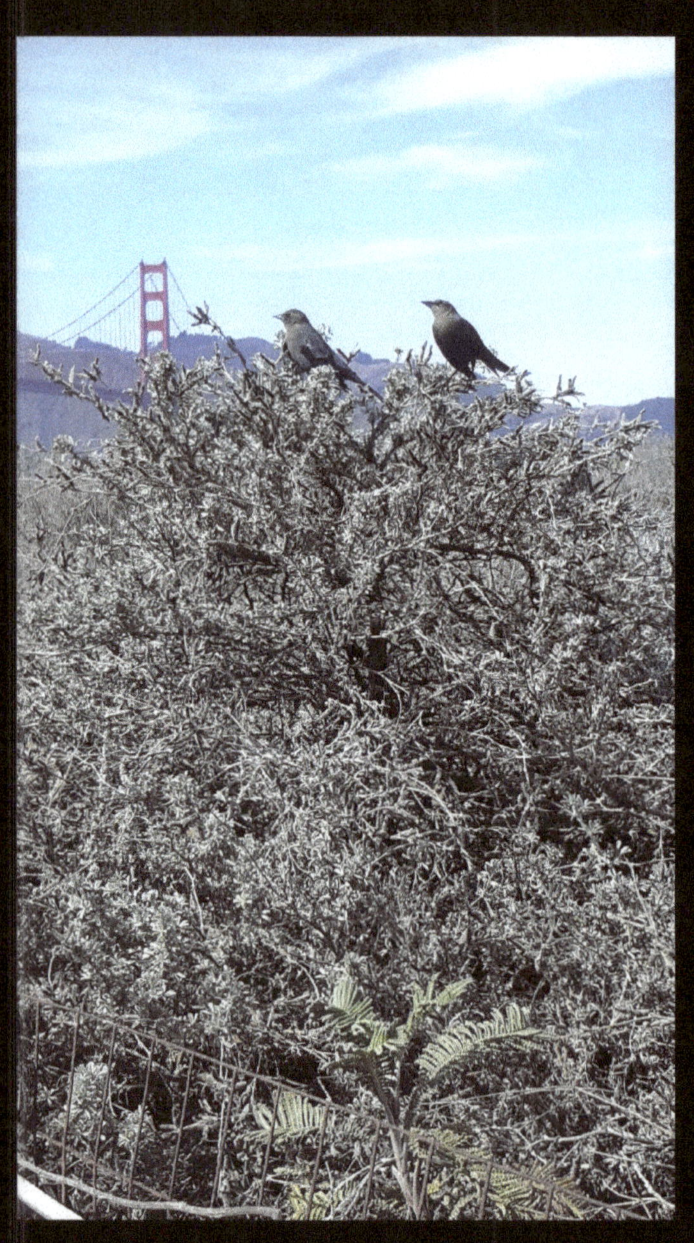
SILVER NITRATE

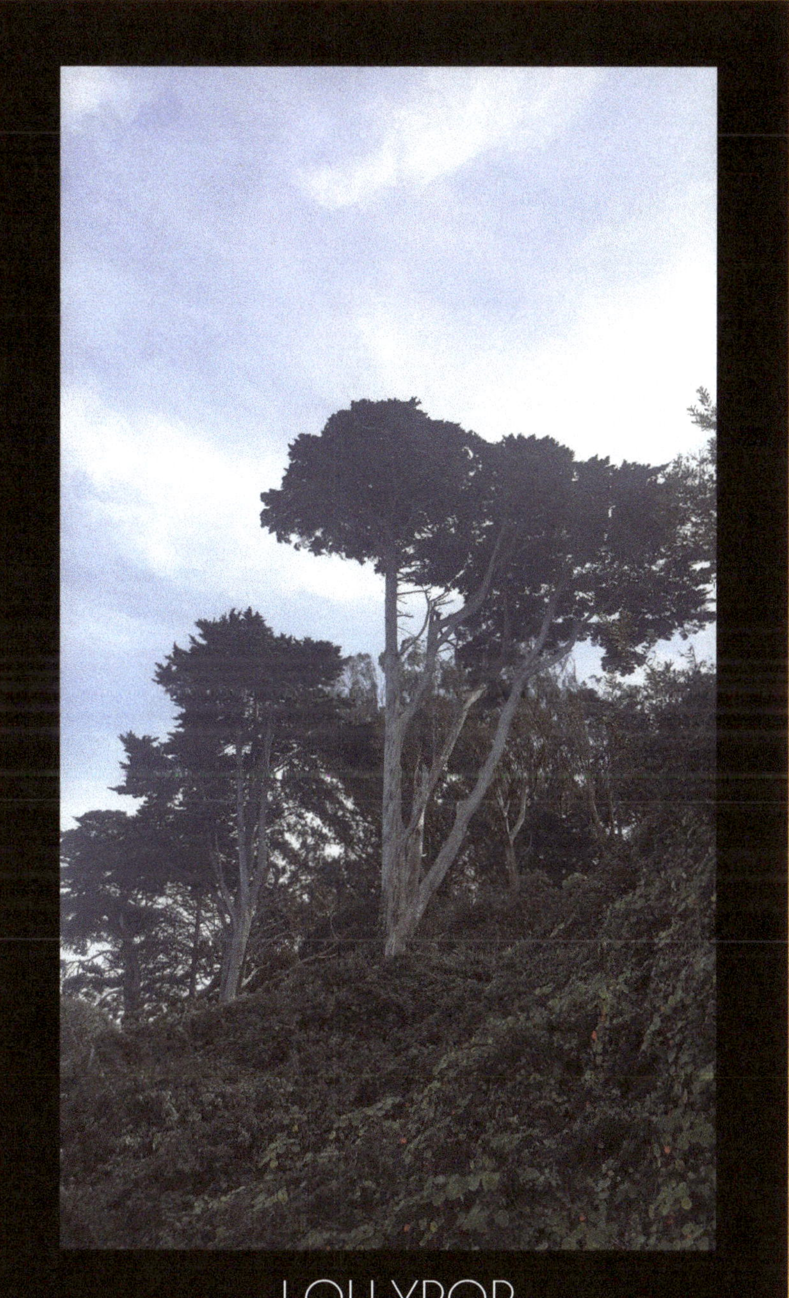

LOLLYPOP

PASSAGES

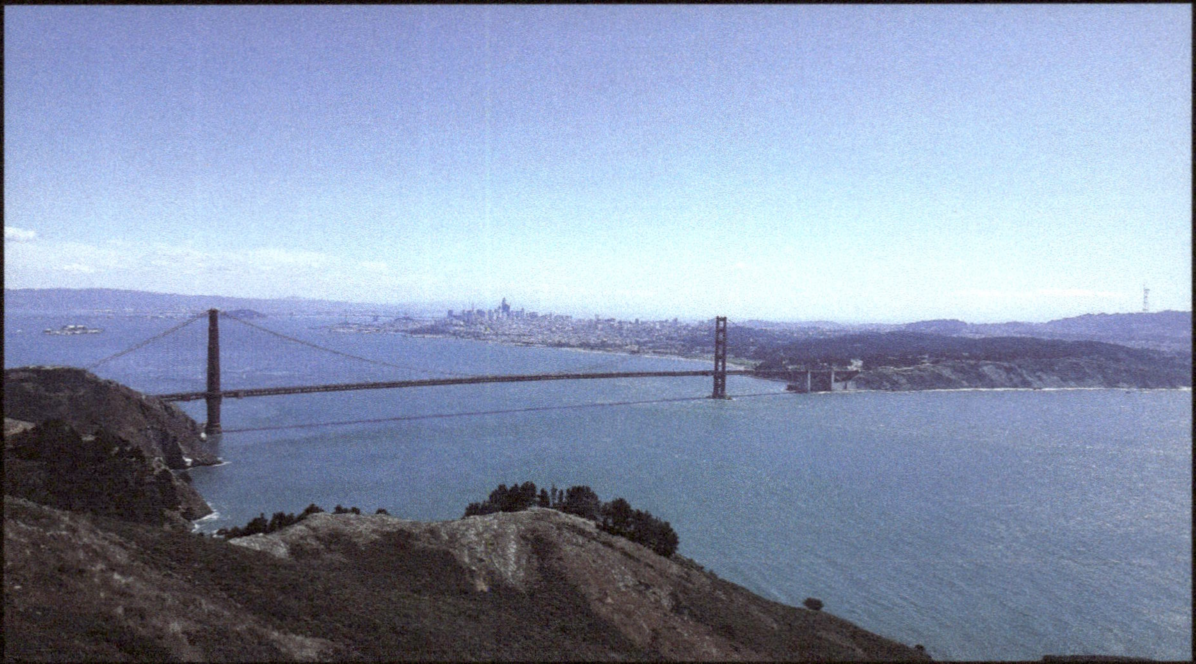

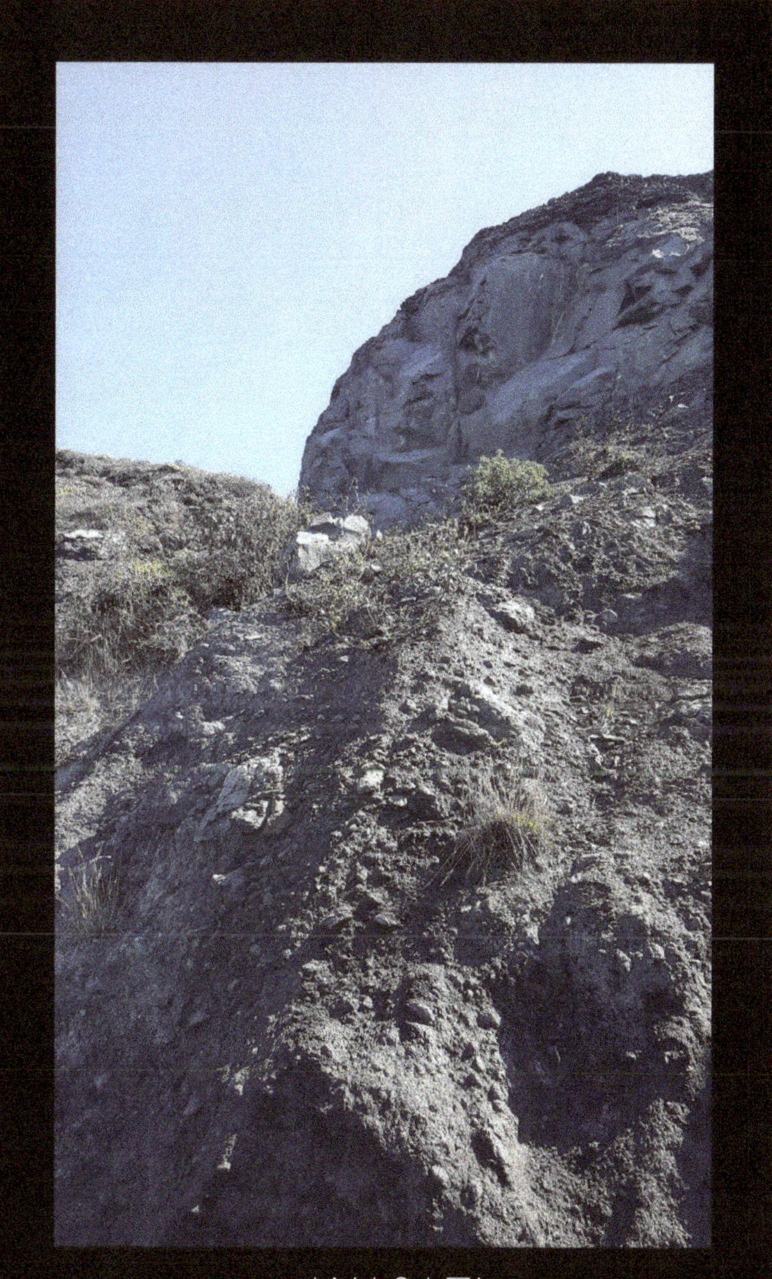

ANASAZI

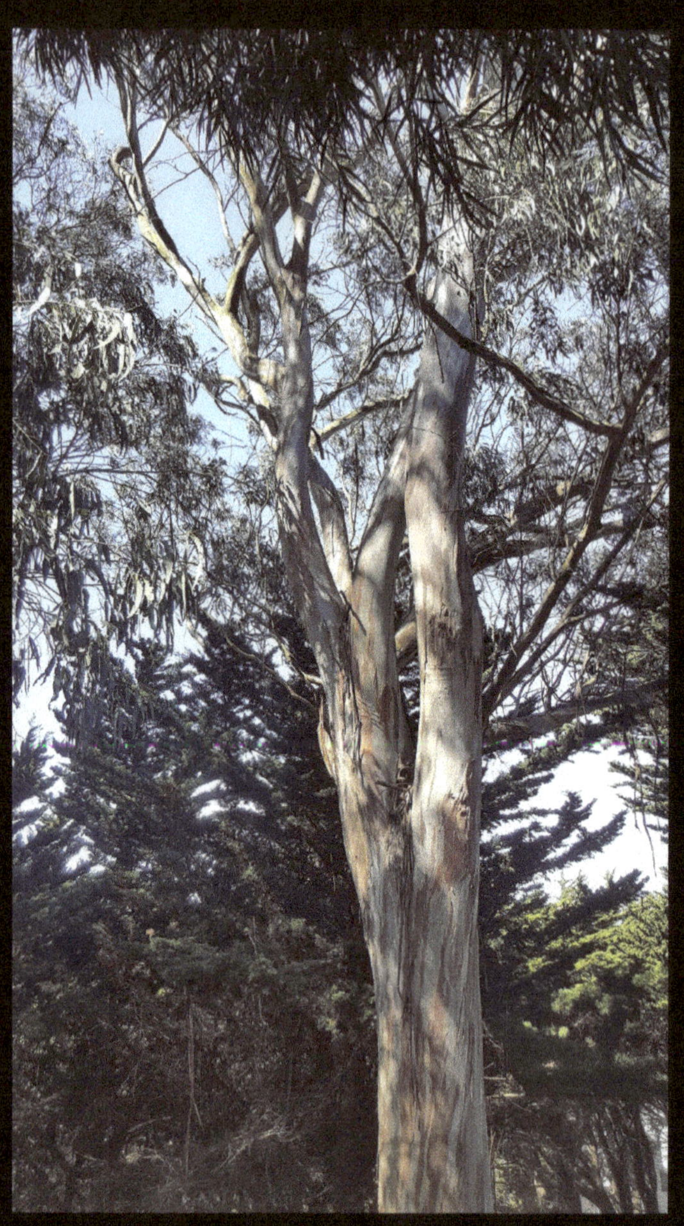

FUZZ

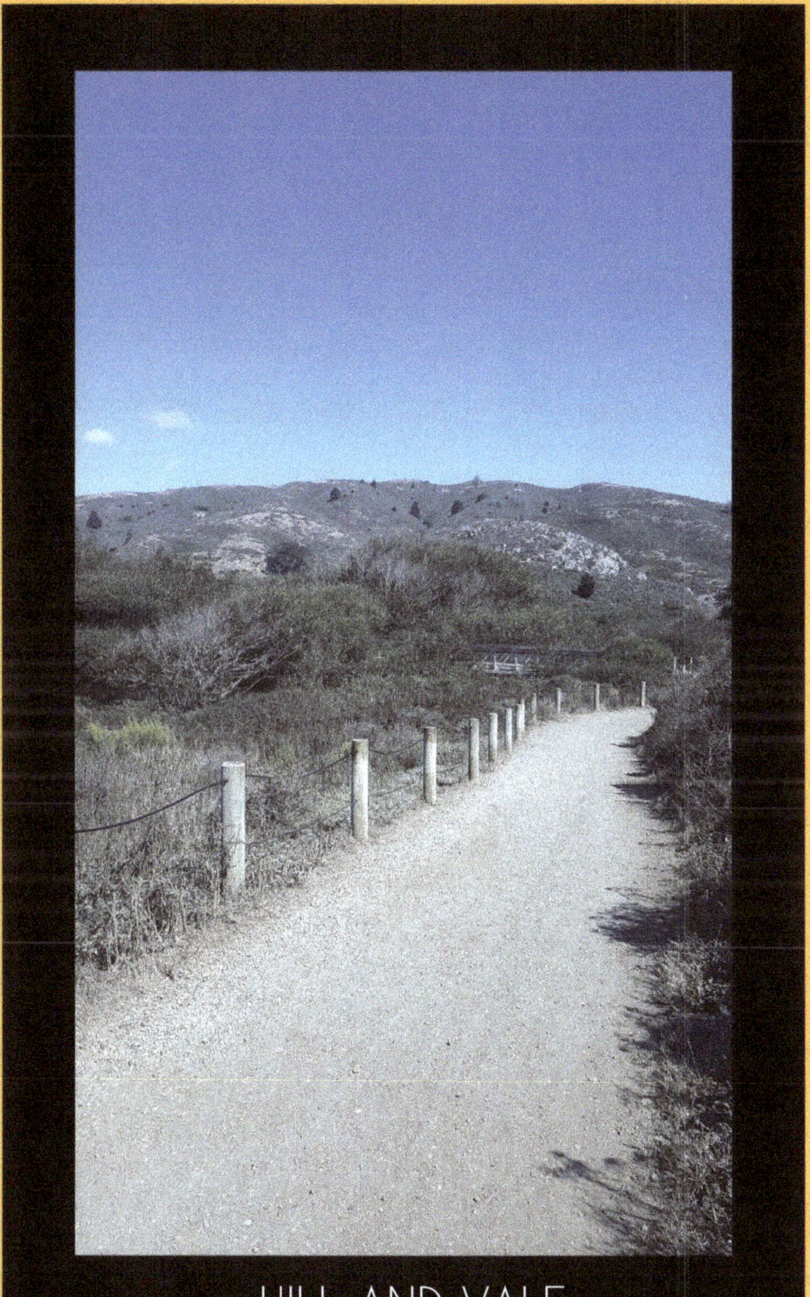

HILL AND VALE

ANCHORS

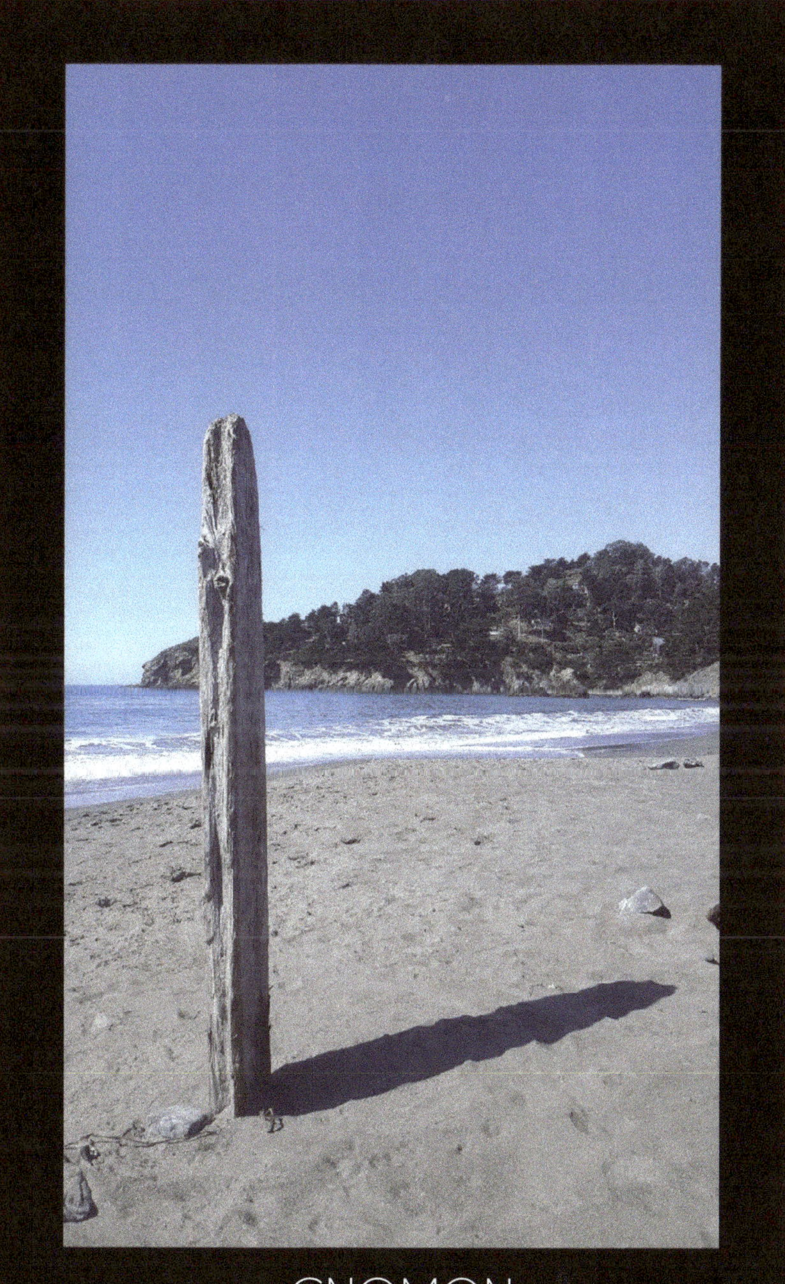

GNOMON

MOB SCENE

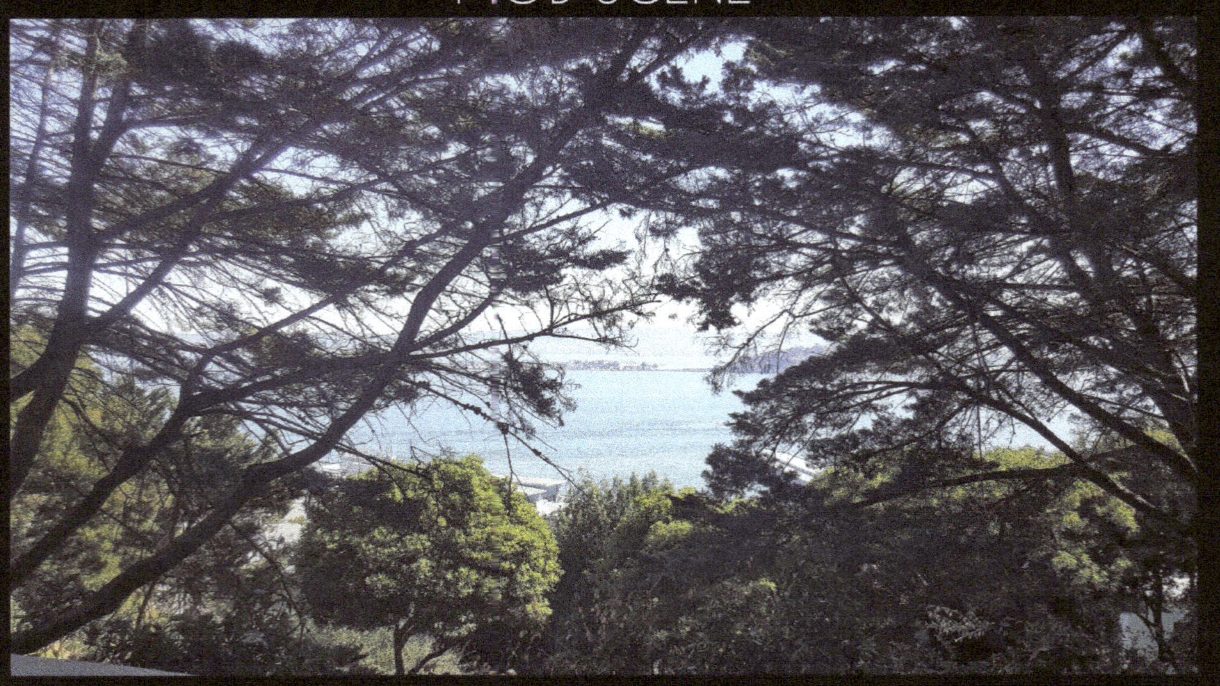

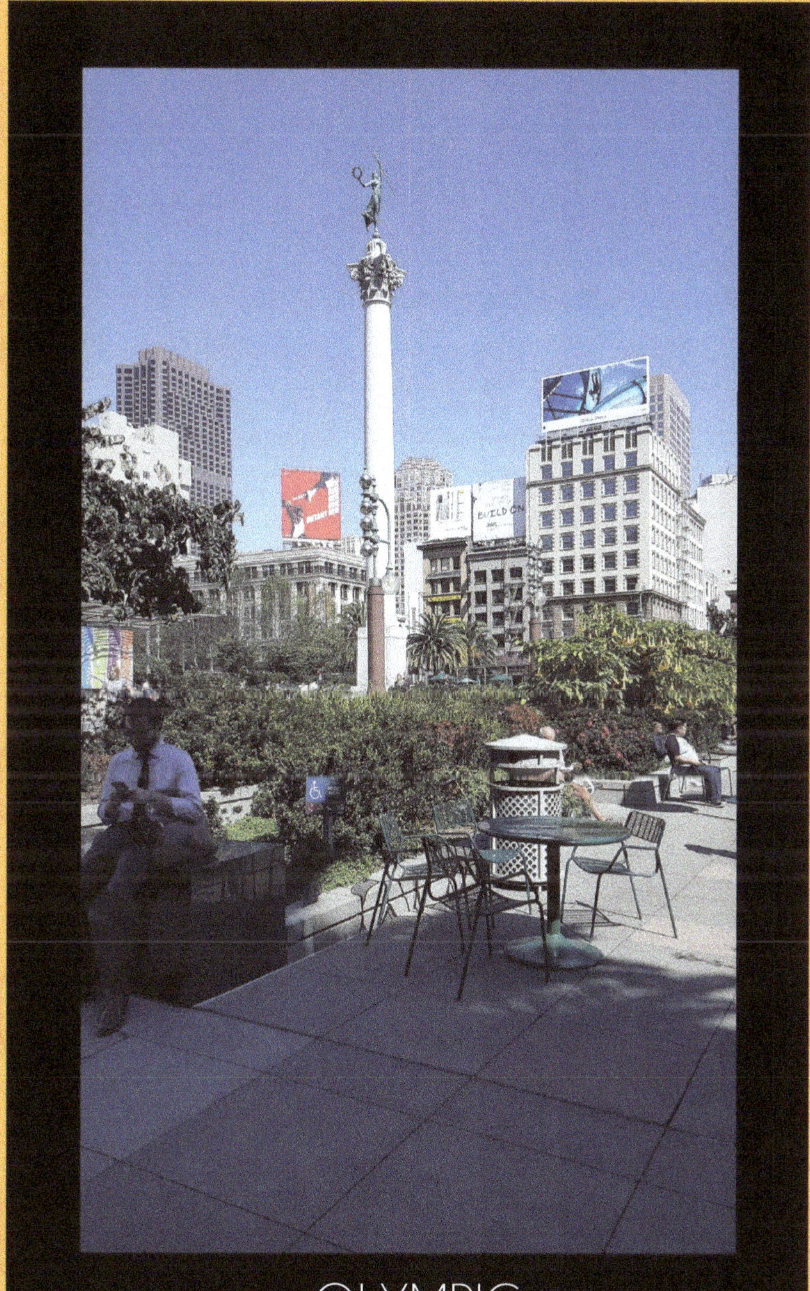

OLYMPIC

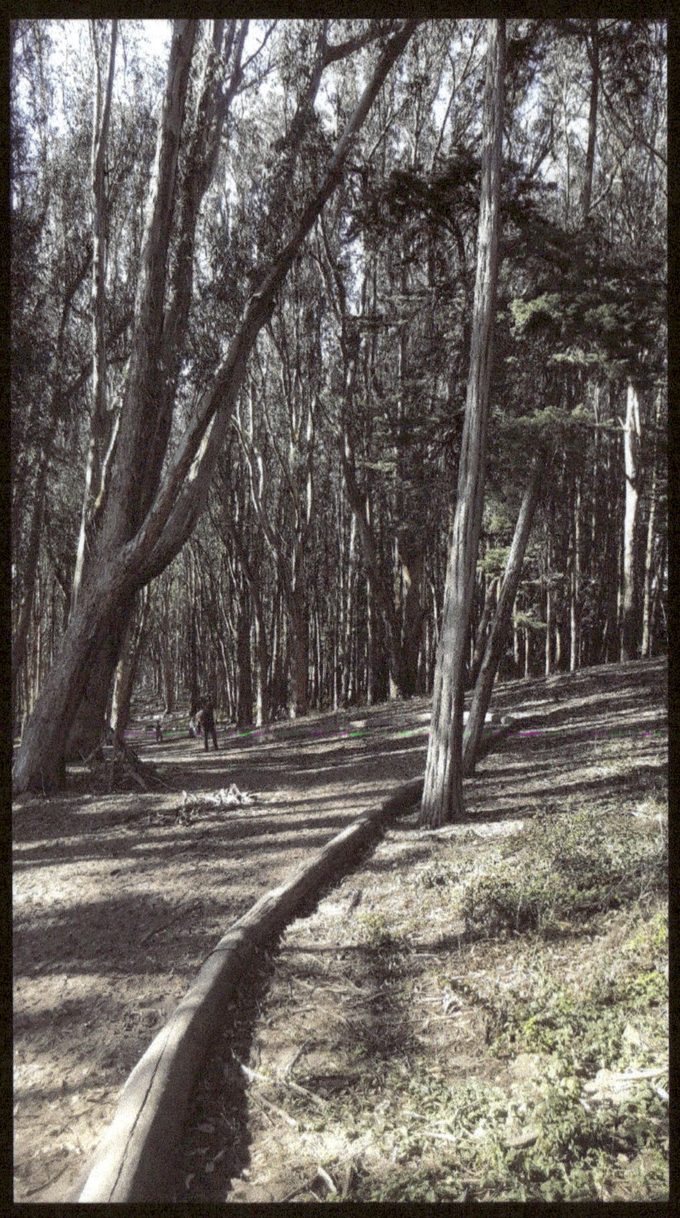

SHADOW LINE

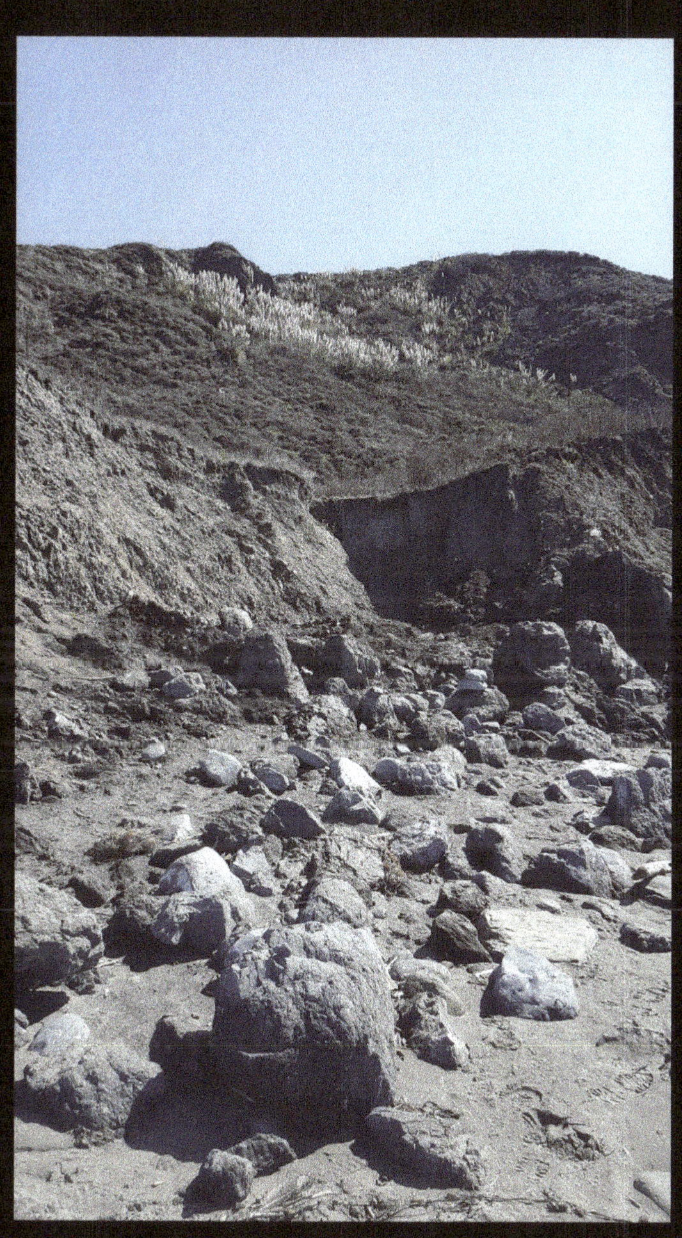

PEBBLED

TOPOGRAPHIC

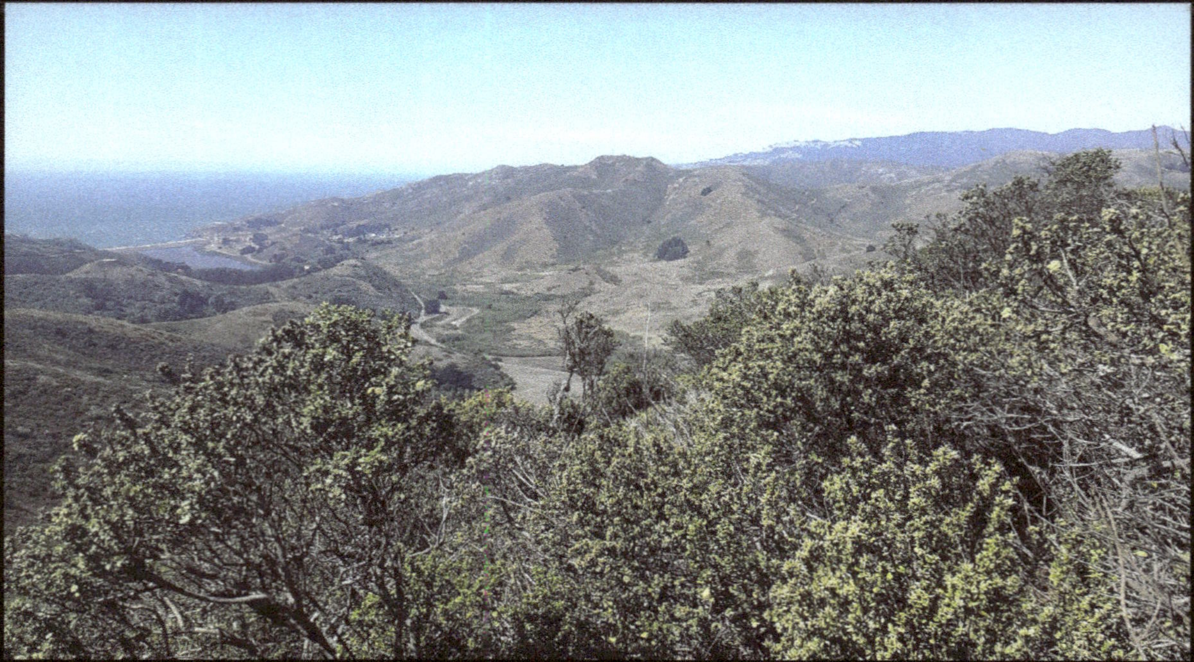

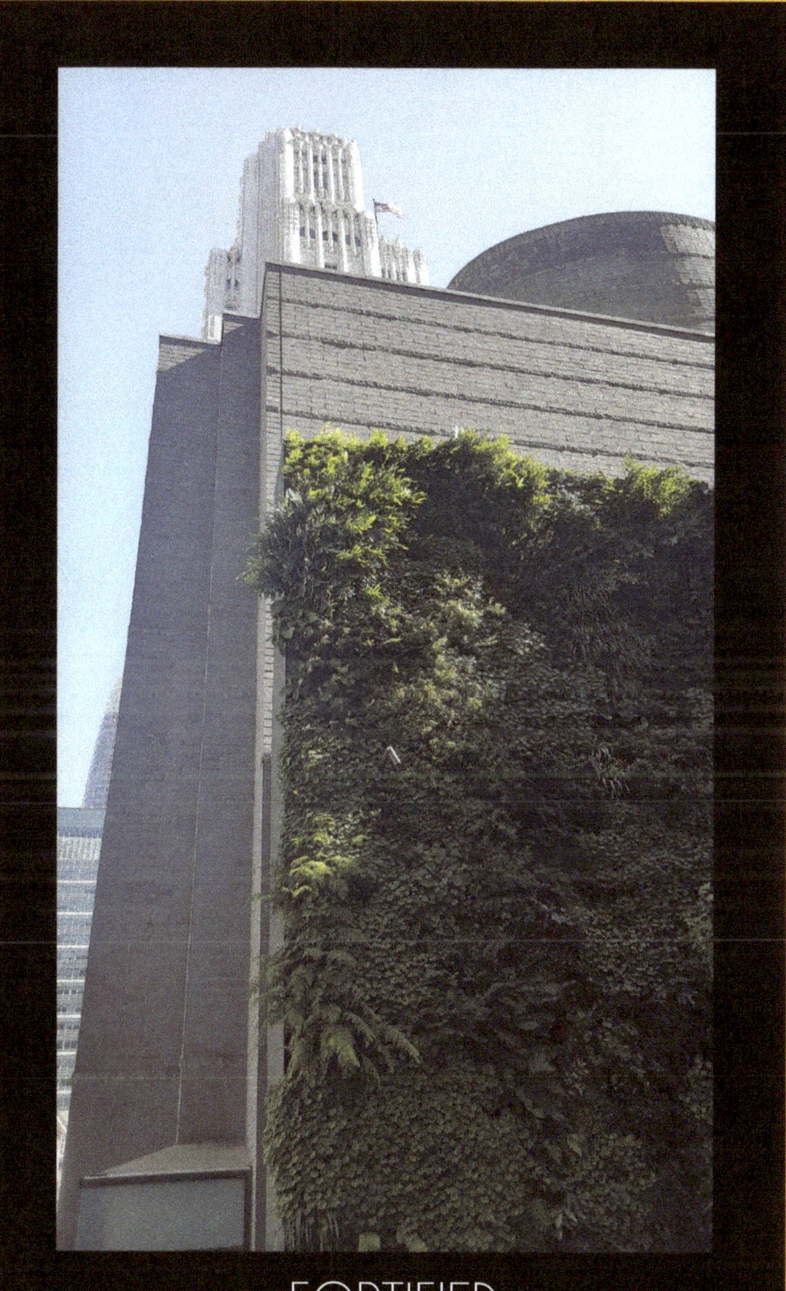

FORTIFIED

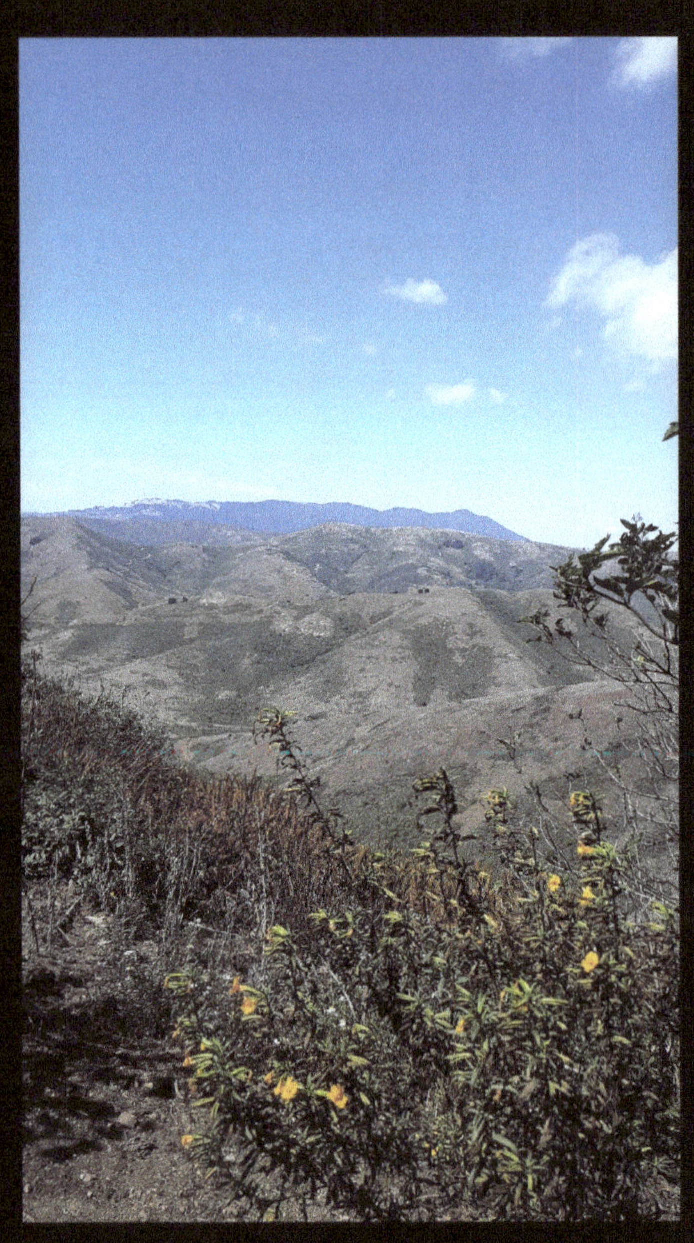
CANARIES

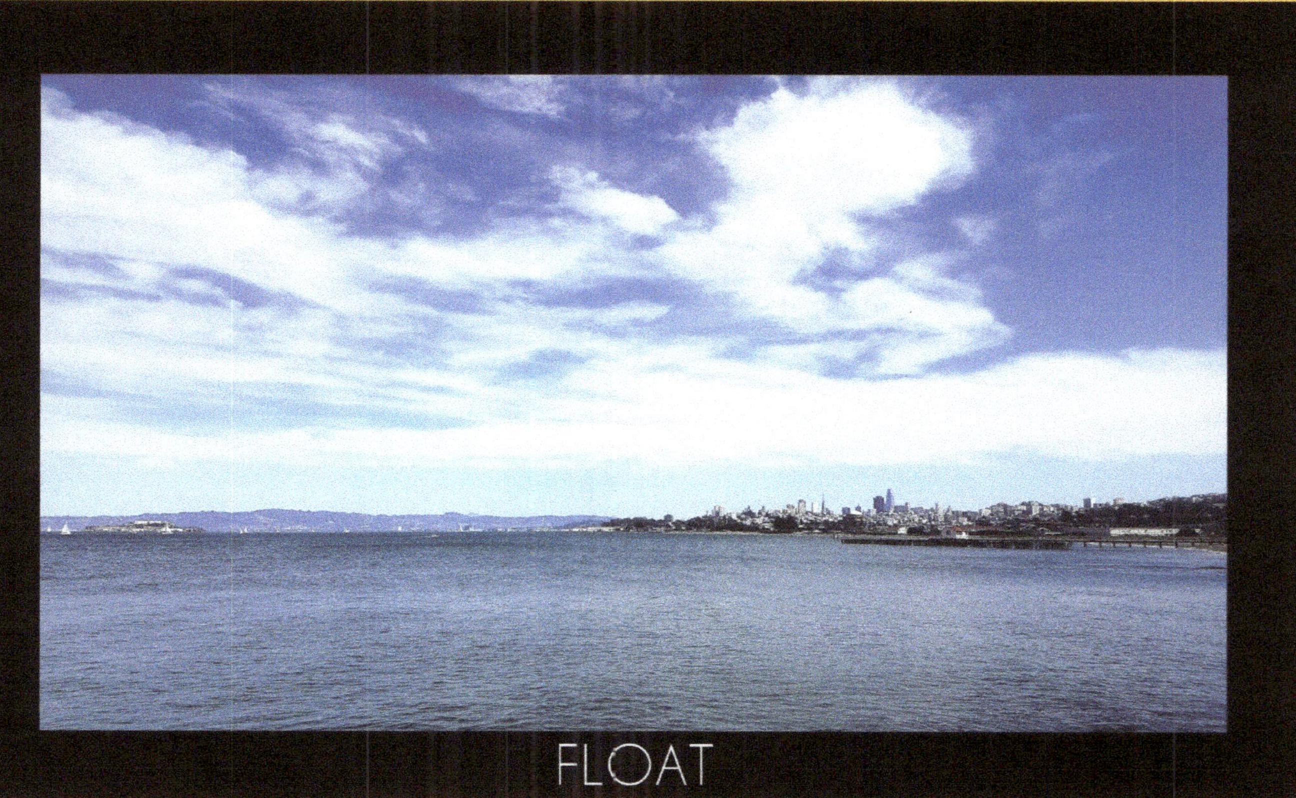
FLOAT

TICKLE

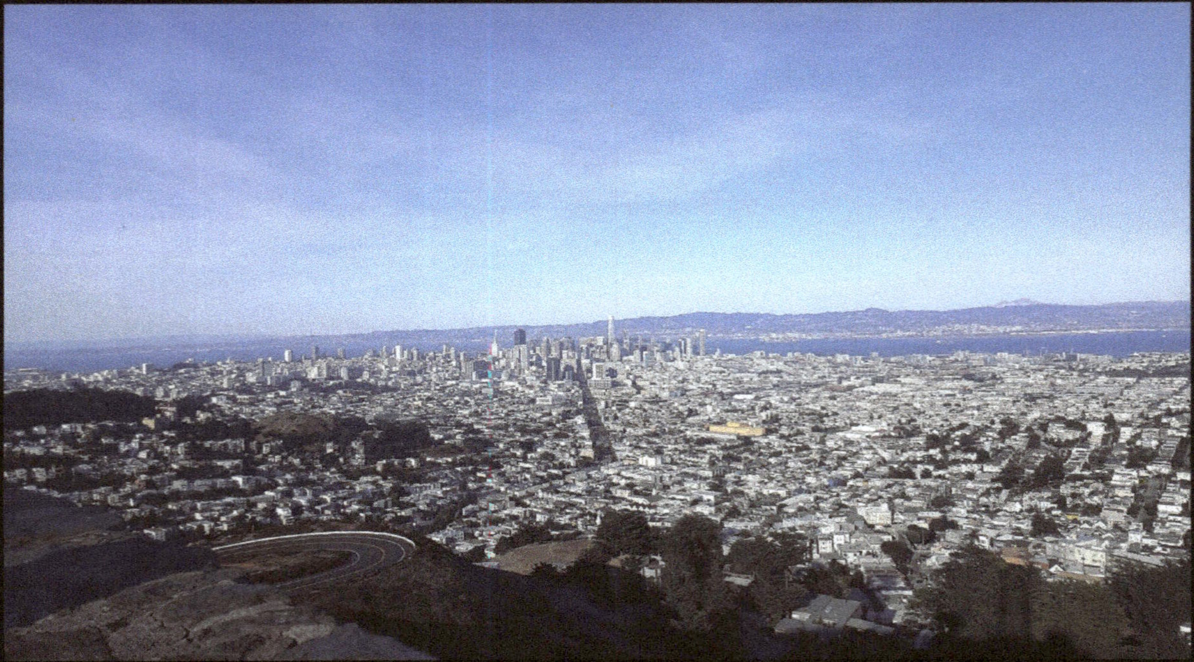

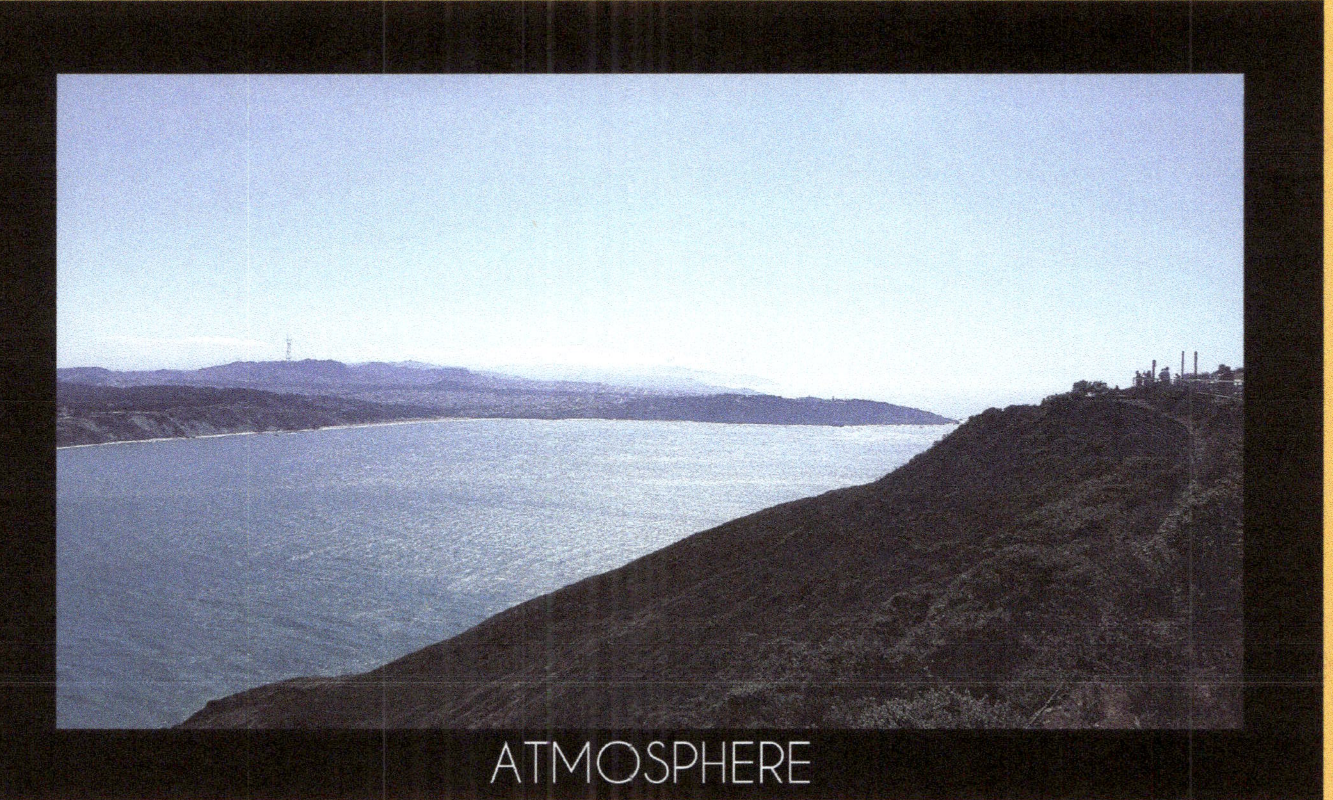
ATMOSPHERE

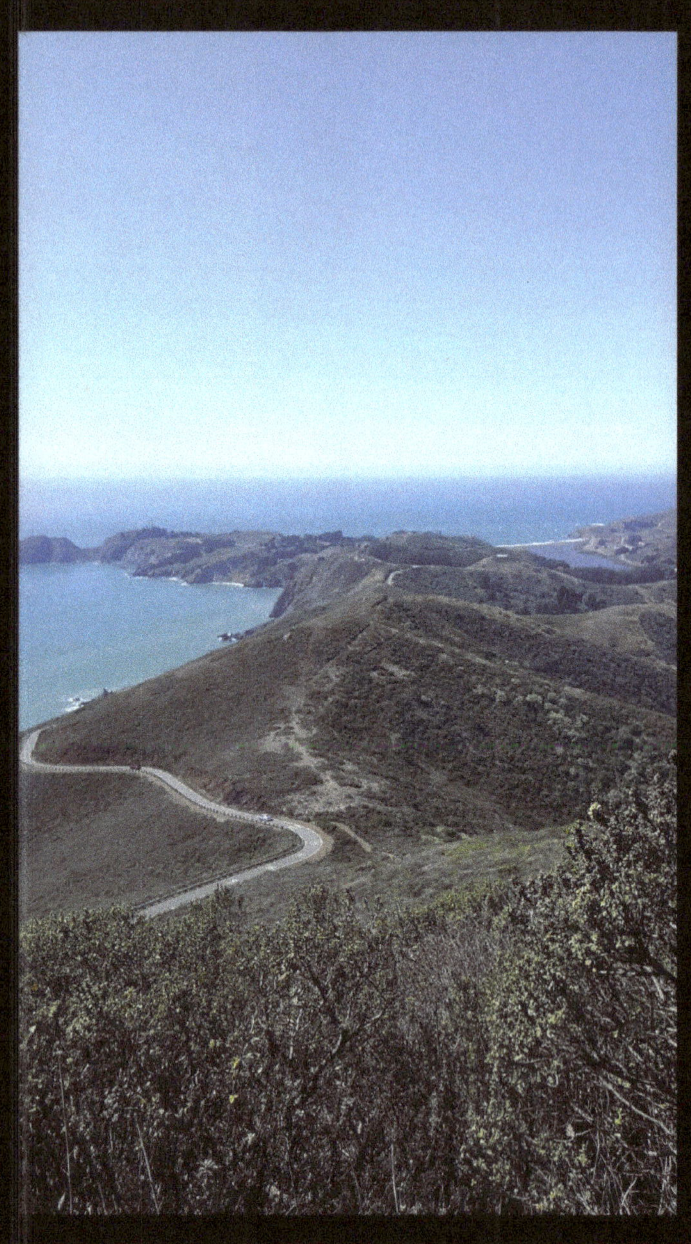

SHETLAND

About the Author

Laine Cunningham's books take readers on adventures around the world. *The Family Made of Dust* is set in the Australian Outback, while *Reparation* is a novel of the American Great Plains. Her women's travel adventure memoir *Woman Alone: A Six-Month Journey Through the Australian Outback* appeals to fans of *Wild* and *Eat Pray Love*.

Fiction

The Family Made of Dust

Beloved

Reparation

Nonfiction

Woman Alone

On the Wallaby Track: Australian Words and Phrases

Seven Sisters: Messages from Aboriginal Australia

Writing While Female or Black or Gay

The Zen of Travel
The Zen of Gardening
Zen in the Stable
The Zen of Chocolate
The Zen of Dogs

The Wisdom of Puppies
The Wisdom of Babies
The Wisdom of Weddings

Bikes of Berlin
Necropolises of New Orleans I & II
Ruins of Rome I & II
Ancients of Assisi I & II
Panoramas of Portugal
Nuances of New York
Glimpses of Germany
Impressions of Italy
Altitudes of the Alps
Knights Through the Ages
Coast of California
Utopia of the Unicorn